YOUR FUTURE IS DECIDED BY YOUR DESIRE TO GO GET IT. SO GO.

FRANK KNIGHT
DO ME
(FEATURING E-HUSTLE)
PRODUCED BY: JUNEDOCC A.K.A. TRIPLE 7
I'M EVERYWHERE
CLICK HERE
SCAN ME
CLICK TO LISTEN
ALL ELEMENTS

TABLE OF
CONTENTS

Artwork by: @0dsev

SCAN ALL QR CODES AND CLICK LINKS TO GET IN ON THE ACTION

BK

BOKANG MASUNYANE

ONE MAN
ONE FIGHT

Said to be one the most exciting and explosive flyweight MMA fighters, Bokang has been dominating One Championship for the past couple of years and is looking to grab a hold of a championship belt.

Originally from South Africa, Bokang began wrestling at the young age of seven. He then began elevating his game and quickly rose to a more competitive level.

He made his amateur debut as a mixed martial artist in 2015 going on a 6 fight win streak. Fighting in Japan soon after, and putting on an exceptional display of martial arts. Masunyane went on to sign with One Championship, to take his game to the next level.

He has won many championships, including a national level and 2 African level championships. He is currently on a streak of 14 wins, which means he hasnt lost a single match in his last 14 matches.

Bokang looks to become MMA's first champion born in Africa and raised in Africa. And with his dynamic fighting style we see that milestone being completed within years to come.

Artwork by: @0dsev

WARRIOR WEEKLY | 07

*CLICK HERE TO
SEE BOKANG IN
ACTION!*

TOP 7 POST PANDEMIC TIPS

TO INCREASE YOUR MENTAL & PHYSICAL HEALTH

01 MENTAL HEALTH

I am an avid reader, and as such, I find that reading uplifting books helps me immensely. Following are just a few of the books from my extensive library that have kept me mentally fit.:

I-Mind Gym – Author Gary Mack & David Casstevens:
"Confidence comes from the emotional Knowing that you are prepared Mentally as well as Physically. Over-prepare so that you do not under perform"

-Can't Hurt Me – Author Gary Goggins
My Favorite Chapters:
- "It's not about a Trophy"
- "The Most Powerful Weapon"
- "Uncommon Amongst Uncommon"
- "The Empowerment of Failure"
"Master your Mind and defy the Odds"

02 PHYSICAL HEALTH

Regular exercise helped me to cope with and avoid COVID Fatigue. Although the Gyms were closed, I was determined to continue my training. I always maintained my own workout paraphernalia: Dumbbells, Pull up/AB Machine, Water Bag, etc.

03 SLEEP

Do not forget Sleep. It is the best meditation. I am in bed by 9 /10 PM every night and awake at 3.30 am every morning focused and ready to make the best of my day, even though I was living through "a new normal" due to the pandemic.

04 AVOID DEPRESSION

I stopped watching the news, and I did not allow others to drag me down with depressing conversations. Staying active, developing positive thoughts, and consistently looking for ways to create and maintain good life habits, is mandatory when navigating a pandemic. For example, Wifey and I regularly took walks in the evenings, played games (Monopoly, Chess, etc.).

WRITTEN BY

GM ABDUL SHABAZZ

05 HEALTHY EATING

All things in moderation! Keeping in mind that no two people are the same, I encourage everyone to determine what works best for them. Personally, I have always tried to avoid sugary drinks, calorie packed deserts, etc. I drink plenty of water all day every day!! Fortunately, I did not have to change my eating habits very much because I've generally always eaten healthy.

06 LAUGHTER IS GOOD FOR THE SOUL

Last but not least, before I went to bed each night, my wife and I would watch some sort of comedy. I found that I went to bed with a smile on my face and woke up in good spirits, despite pandemic woes!! This continues to this day.

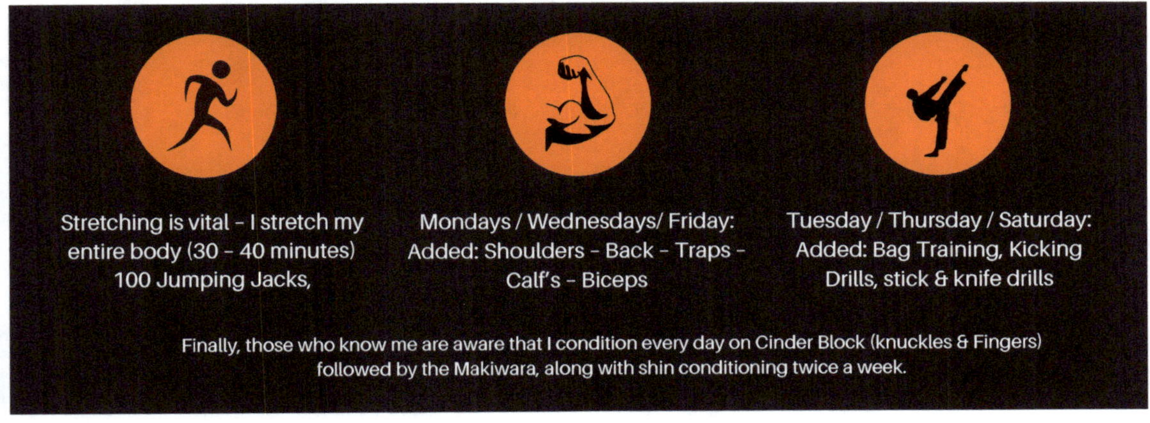

UPCOMING

MMA FIGHTS

UFC Fight Night: Kattar vs. Emmett
Moody Center, Austin, TX
Jun 24
5:30 PM

2022 PFL Regular Season: Featherweights &
Heavyweights
OTE Arena, Atlanta, GA

Jun 24
6:00 PM
Bellator 282: Mousasi vs. Eblen
Mohegan Sun Arena, Uncasville, CT

Jun 25
1:00 PM
CW 140: Cage Warriors 140
SSE Arena (NIR), Belfast

BOXING FIGHTS

July 16: Los Angeles (DAZN) -- Ryan Garcia
vs. Javier Fortuna, 12 rounds, lightweights

July 23: Saudi Arabia (DAZN -- Title fight:
Oleksandr Usyk vs. Anthony Joshua, 12
rounds, for Usyk's WBA, WBO and IBF
heavyweight titles

July 30: Brooklyn, New York (Showtime) --
Danny Garcia vs. Jose Benavidez Jr., 12
rounds, junior middleweights

Aug. 13: TBA, Florida (ESPN/ESPN+) --
Teofimo Lopez vs. Pedro Campa, 10 rounds,
junior welterweights

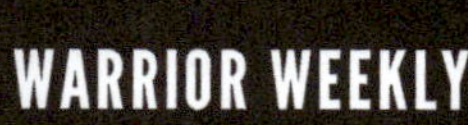

LIVE STREAM
WARRIOR
WEEKLY
V/S
ONLINE
SPORTS
BETTING
COMING SOON
FREE TO SIGN UP | MMA BOXING
GET PRIZES EVEN WHEN YOU
LOSE!
BROUGHT TO YOU BY
DEADLYARTOFSURVIVAL.COM

Question & Answer

One of Kung fu's Top Fighters

Type something…

SIFU RALPH MITCHELL

Well, I got started actually back in late 65/66. I joined a judo school. That was my first entry into martial arts, cuz you know, the usual story too small, too short for basketball, football type of thing. I lived in Harlem in a project so, you know, It was pretty hard trying to find my niche at that young age, but I, I went to a judo school in the area and that, that was it for me.

I found my game. Yes, it was judo. And then a few years later, I went down Chinatown with my cousin who knows your father. My cousin is, Teddy Sampson, he lived in the Smith houses. Your dad knows him very well. It was actually Teddy that hooked me up with your father.

I started learning, going Fu at the same time I was doing judo in Chinatown, New York on uh, 51 east Broadway. Okay. So Kung Fu took. Well, I did both, but okay. I, I can tell you, I GOM Fu became my lifestyle. Okay. All right.

Describe how was training in your era as compared to training in today's era?

Wow. Well, first of all, back in the day, there were no signs up. Now you gotta understand the Chinatown situation. They just open up their school for non-Chinese and up until then, no non-Chinese were learning your art in Chinatown, New York, because. All the Chinese signs, you know, they were in Chinese and they weren't open to change that, to teach non Chinese yet.

I know, but fast forward, I was one of the first non-Chinese to join that club. And I gotta give props again to my cousin, it was Teddy who took me down there because my Si fu lived in this same project building that Teddy lived in.

Oh, wow. Yeah. So, you know, it, it was like hook me up. So as far as what was the difference in training back in the day? You know, learning Kung Fu first of all, there was a major Chinese English problem. Mm-hmm so basically the second in command was the one who was breaking it down for us. Because he had just graduated from Seward park high school.

But coming up there was no backtalk or nothing. Oh no, no, no, nothing, nothing you didn't say. Well, could you show me that again? No, no, nah. Ain't happening. It was tough. Love, lots of pushups, sit ups, you know, standing in the horse stances, you know, they're punching your legs and stuff, trying to break you.

but, um, I wasn't gonna give up, I was gonna deal with whatever the torture they gave us because I knew this was it. Now fast forward you got Jacoby and Myers lawyers. Oh yeah. And as you know, and you know, and the whole martial law game has changed, you know, because of the sport concept versus just strictly self defense.

Q: Who was your toughest fight?

Well, to be honest with you, all my full contact fights were tough fights. They were tough because, it was anything goes back in those days and the judges. You didn't have a understanding of what was legal or not illegal. You know what I mean? Right. So to be honest, the hardest part of my training was the preparation, because I had to learn and rather fight with people.

So you know, it was just good karma attracts good karma. You know, they gave me tough love. Right. And being that, you know, I was a lightweight, you know, 130, 1 31 pounds, you know, But they, they respected my perseverance.
Excuse my. Especially in the karate versus kung fu tournaments.

I was fighting guys that were heavier than me always. Right. But to me it was no big deal because all of my mentors and sparring partners. Big and heavyweight and, you know, that's the way it was back in the early days, right.

There was no weight classes, so it wasn't uncommon. So I had to represent my art, dealing with the people I mentioned, you know they set me straight, but they respected my skill base. And also, you know, I just wasn't kicking, punching. I was doing the Kung Fu sweeps.

I actually was incorporating judo concepts throws. And I was well rounded, you know, myself and my other contemporaries, we were the, the original MMA people. Right.

We called ourselves combat athletes because we just didn't train, just, you know, doing forms and stuff. We were jogging, we were doing sit ups. We were jumping rope. Right. You had to be well rounded and especially with the type of people I was fighting and to including your, your father. I had to cover all the bases. So, you know, but to say truthfully, who was my hardest fight, no, the hardest fights were in preparation for the full contact matches. They always say the, the preparation is like 90%, right. Of the toughest part of the fight. You gotta train. you know, and you have to train, right?

A lot of, uh, the Kung Fu systems, there was no cardiovascular training and they, they weren't geared for fighting in tournament. It was just for self defense, right. All due respects. So I had to find people. Mention who played outside that game of just forms and a lot of specificity training developing my skill set.

How has Martial Arts changed your life?

Well, martial arts was my drug of choice. Cuz when I got out of military much less Vietnam, you know, it was either drugs, alcohol or suicide.

I chose the way of the warrior as I did in Vietnam. Just get back into martial arts, get back into Chinatown, get back into my Kung fu and I was training brother. I can tell you I was training five days a week. Hardcore, because I had to fight the demons of the war that was in my mind.

That was my drug right there. Martial arts, and that's what changed my life.

INGRAM TAXES

ACCOUNTING & BUSINESS MANAGEMENT

FOR RECORDING ARTISTS, ENTERTAINERS, AND ATHLETES

CELEB

Budgeting for video shoots, tours, and shows.

- Bookkeeping: manage daily transactions
- Payroll: Management of payroll and taxes
- Payables & Receivables: Management of supplier and customer invoices

Tax Audits, which includes overseas Vat Tax.

for more information, visit www.ingramtaxes.com

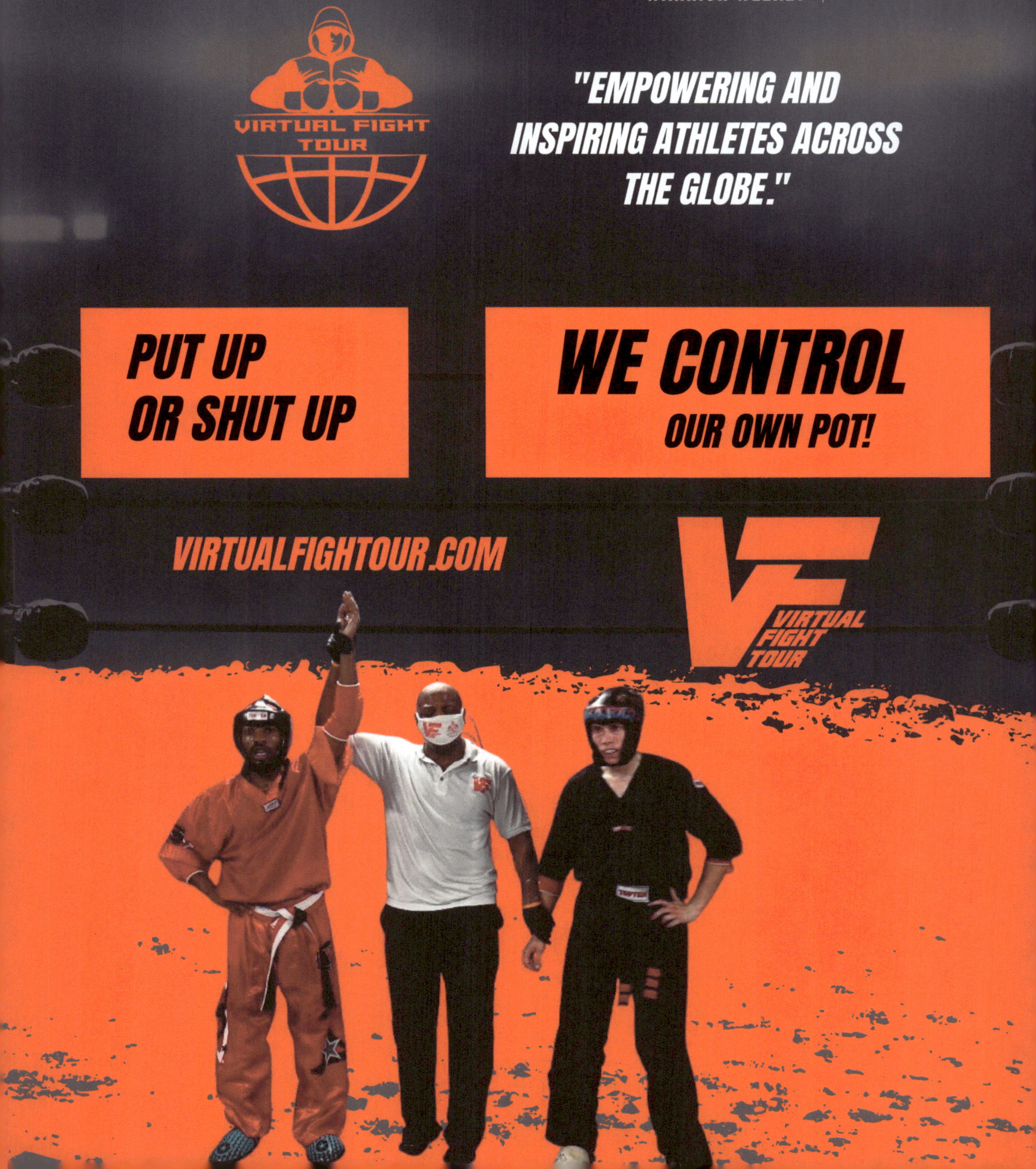
VIRTUAL FIGHT TOUR
"EMPOWERING AND INSPIRING ATHLETES ACROSS THE GLOBE."
PUT UP OR SHUT UP
WE CONTROL OUR OWN POT!
VIRTUALFIGHTOUR.COM
VIRTUAL FIGHT TOUR

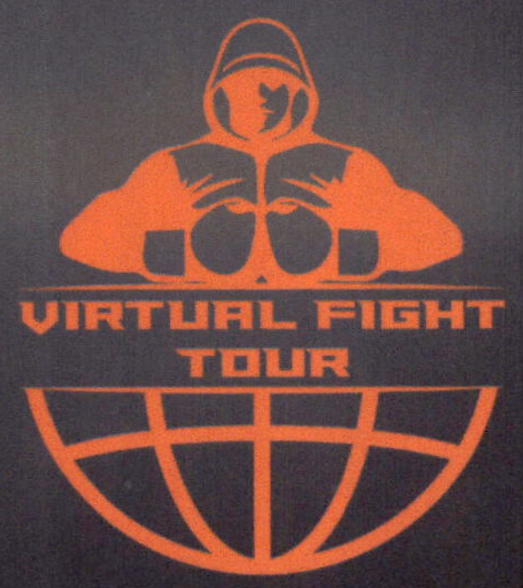

2000 F 8.0   M   D45/2.8 120
43
TRA

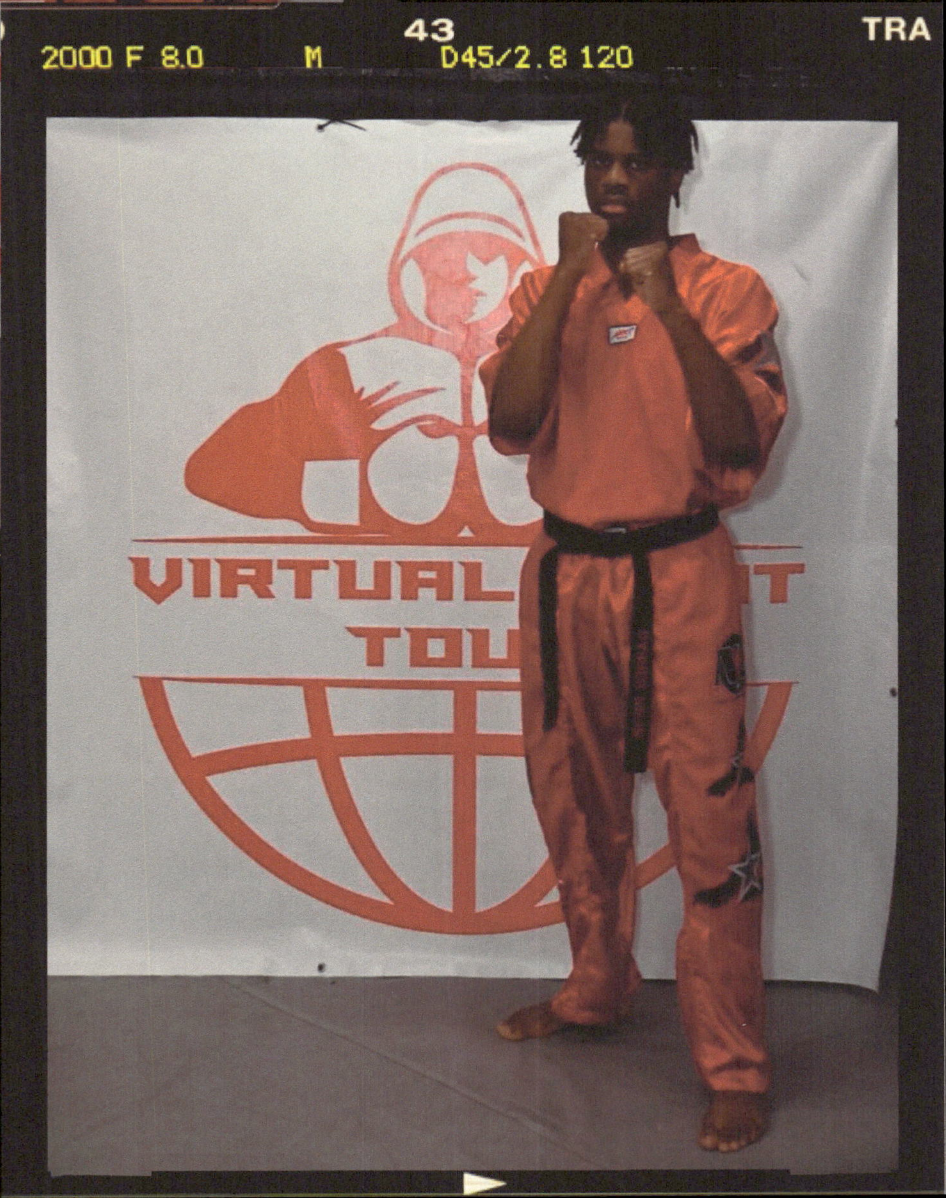

VIRTUAL FIGHT
TOUR

TRAP
GAMBINO
FIGHTER
He has something to prove.
WARRIOR WEEKLY MMA 19
MMA

HIS JOURNEY TO THE TOP

Trap Gambino is an actor, rapper, and aspiring mixed martial artist, by way of Las Vegas, Nevada. Trap has made appearances on multiple shows, one in particular the reality TV show "The Dr. Phil Show". His appearance on the show fueled his dream to become an established MMA fighter. Since then he has lost over 100 pounds and is currently preparing for his next fight.

Gambino plans to compete in the super heavyweight division, and has recently sign to Rize Fighting Championship. A popular cage fighting league hosted throughout the U.S It's just the beginning for Trap Gambino, so make sure you tune in. Either way youll be seeing a lot more of Trap in the future.

Trap Gambino ground and pounding his opponent.

Beating adversity and facing the odds.

Rollerz
High
Rollerz
RJJ
ROCK
TYSON
R/O
ORIGINALS
FAMILY FARMS

SHAOLIN

KUNG FU IS FLEXIBLE

Here when we use the word flexible the meaning is a bit abstract. Flexibility can take on several meanings when it pertains to the Art of the Shaolin Temple. Of course, there is the physical flexibility which comes from the Shaolin Ya Tui {stretching routine}. The physical stretches done in Shaolin Kung Fu are not only done for the sake of performing high kicks, but to make the body nimble, agile, and quick. Not to mention the many health benefits that come along with having a flexible body. Many of The Shaolin Ji Ben Gong {basics} build upon the flexibility gained from the Ya Tui routine and further develop a flexible agile body.

Going deeper into the topic we have the flexibility of the applications found within the many solo routines and forms of traditional Shaolin Kung Fu. As a starter to understand how kung fu can apply to self-protection we must take a look at the training methods. There is a great misunderstanding that comes from the belief that when a Kung Fu Practitioner uses his skills for defense it should look identical to the forms. This may in part do to the exaggerated nature of the famous kung fu theater films made popular in the 1970s and 80s. In reality the forms are exaggerated motions for conditioning purposes. Wide stances develop leg strength. Wide open movement teach body coordination and power development. The forms help to train attributes such as balance, coordination, agility, speed all while building the students stamina.

Besides training the Kung Fu students attributes they also train specific concepts and strategies.
Shaolin Kung Fu is not a dogmatic system. The movements are fluid and flexible. If one watches for example Tong Bi Quan {a popular Shaolin form} being performed from different Shaolin schools the observer will notice similarities but differences as well. It is the flexibility and fluidness that leads to slight variations from student to student and school to school, this is natural as not all body types are the same. As in Chan Buddhism philosophy life is constantly changing, nothing is static and permanent. We need to be flexible in movements and thoughts, to adapt to the constant change in life and in practice.

A found memory comes to mind when explaining the topic of flexible applications. It was during the time of the famous Chinese celebration called Guo Nian {Chinese New Year} A time when the students go home for a long break. The holiday takes place in the dead of winter and my wife, and I happened to be living in the mountainous area of Shaolin in the area known as Songshan Shaolin. My Shifu {Shi Yan Shuang} was staying in the mountains along with his wife {Shi Niang}, and the grounds and streets were pretty much desolate. Training in the courtyard with snow on the ground my wife and I went through the movements of the Pon Long Dao {Swimming Dragon} broad sword form with the watchful eye of our Shifu looking on. After describing a sequence in the form, he picked up a near by two foot stick which I believe to be a discarded section of an old broom handle. He began to swing the stick around with the movements resembling the form we were learning. {The applications are flexible; you can even use a stick in a similar manner see.} This lesson has stuck with me and is not limited to simply using a stick in the same way you would use a sword. It has a broad spectrum here. On several different occasions my Shifu has mentioned how Shaolin Kung Fu can be used freely and spontaneously without restrictions in its applications for self-protection. In the ever changing and unpredictable world anything can happen and having a flexible attitude can save one's skin.

Flexibility of the mind is equally as important as flexibility of the body. In Buddhist beliefs everything is impermanent and every changing. The pupil is taught to not think in a ridged way. To be nonjudgement and free flowing. This can be a very useful tool in dealing with day-to-day stress that is unavoidable. Even monks in a temple have stress in their lives. In fact, even living creature is exposed to stress and hard times, no one or thing is free from its grasp. In having a flexible mind, we can learn to accept that which we cannot change or avoid. Learn from difficult experiences and grow from them. By not attaching and clinging to preconceived ideas we can handle what life throws at us with a peaceful mind. One method for training the mind is through meditation, which helps us calm the mind and focus in the present.
To truly understand Shaolin Kung Fu and its physical, mental, and spiritual teaches we should learn to look outside the box. Our perception on life now may change in five, ten or fifteen years. The methods are used a tool and not a means to an end. To let go be free and in the moment. This is what it means to be truly flexible.

About the writer:

Shi fu Chris Friedman has been doing the martial arts since his early teens. He has earned several black belts and teaching certifications. He lived and trained in China for thirteen years, including living as a foreign disciple in Songshan Shaolin. He now lives in Northern VA teaching Shaolin Kung Fu.

CREATED BY

THE
FUTURE OF
MARTIAL ARTS
CONTENT

JOIN & GET 20% OFF

The DAOS Company started off with it's first publication, the Deadly Art of Survival Magazine. With the latest publication Warrior Weekly, we look to bridge the gap between all fight sports, social media content, art, news, and pop/ hip-hop culture.

www.deadlyartofsurvival.com

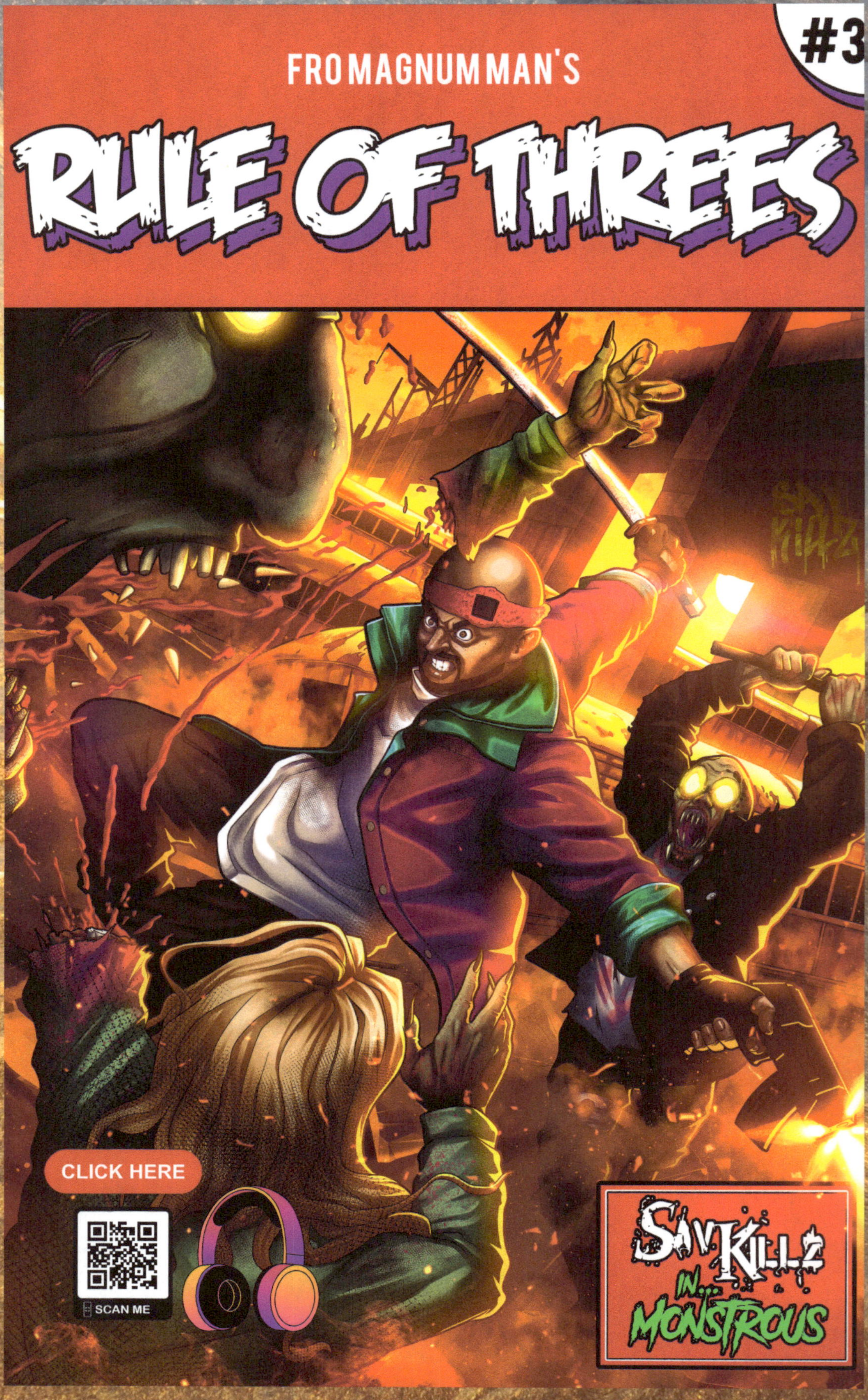

FRO MAGNUM MAN'S
#3
RULE OF THREES
CLICK HERE
SCAN ME
SAV KILLZ
IN...
MONSTROUS